HOW IT WAS WITH DOOMS

A TRUE STORY FROM AFRICA

HOW IT WAS WITH
DOOMS

A TRUE STORY FROM AFRICA

Text and Illustrations
by Xan Hopcraft and Carol Cawthra Hopcraft

ALADDIN PAPERBACKS

New York   London   Toronto   Sydney   Singapore

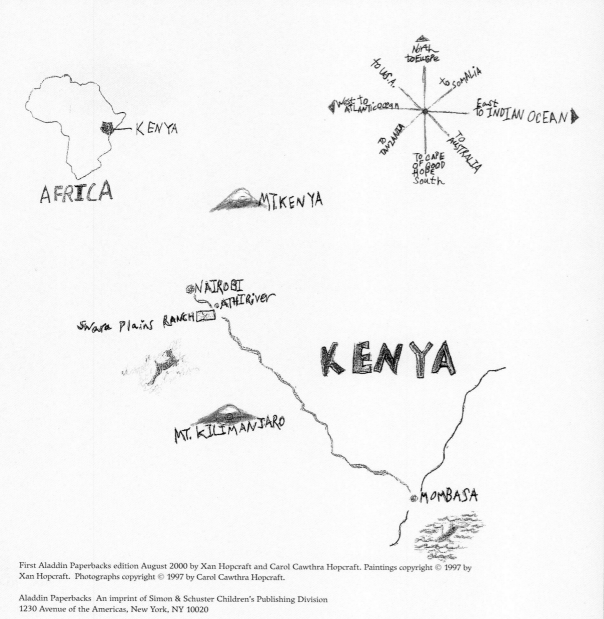

AFRICA

KENYA

MT.KENYA

North
to Europe

to U.S.A.

to SOMALIA

West to
Atlantic ocean

East
to INDIAN OCEAN

to TANZANIA

to AUSTRALIA

TO CAPE
OF
GOOD
HOPE
South

NAIROBI

ATHI River

Swara Plains RANCH

KENYA

MT. KILIMANJARO

MOMBASA

First Aladdin Paperbacks edition August 2000 by Xan Hopcraft and Carol Cawthra Hopcraft. Paintings copyright © 1997 by Xan Hopcraft. Photographs copyright © 1997 by Carol Cawthra Hopcraft.

Aladdin Paperbacks An imprint of Simon & Schuster Children's Publishing Division
1230 Avenue of the Americas, New York, NY 10020

Library of Congress Catalog Card Number: 96-1428
ISBN 0-689-81091-1 (hc.) ISBN 0-689-83539-6 (Aladdin pbk.)

For Doons — who taught us

Dooms

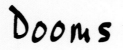

"Dooms" is a nickname for a small boy cheetah.

The name comes from *Duma*, the Swahili word for cheetah.

CONTENTS

About How Dooms Came to Live with Us

When Dooms came, I wasn't born yet. That's why I don't know this part of the story for sure, but I'm telling you the way it was told to me. It's a true story, all of it.

Our House

Dooms came inside the coat of a man looking for a job. There were no jobs, but as the man left, he opened his coat and said, "You wouldn't want this, would you?" and there was Dooms, not much bigger than a regular kitten.

Dooms was all fur and teeth, and he was scared. A real scared cat.

When Dooms is scared, he opens his mouth and puts his head down and looks hard at you. Just stares without moving. He's scared, and you're scared because he looks like he means business.

9

▼▼

Dooms was only three or four weeks old then, and he had no mother or father. That's why he was scared. Scared of loud noises and the smells of other animals, especially human animals like us. Scared in the night when he was alone in the grass, waiting. Waiting for his mother to come back from hunting for his food.

The father cheetah doesn't stay with the mother to help with the cubs. The mother cheetah has to take care of the babies all by herself, and it's a very hard job. That's why Dooms's mother had to leave her cubs to go hunting for food by herself.

The first part of the mother's job, before hunting, is to find a place for the den where the babies will stay when they're too small to move far. Dooms's mother had to find a place with thick grass around it and maybe

hyena hyena your beauty goes, you have the plains to Roam and go, you can be great you can be bad you anyway I like you all like

with rocks as well so the cubs' enemies—snakes, birds that eat animals, jackals, lions, and hyenas—can't find them. It's mostly lions and hyenas that eat cheetah cubs.

And the cubs are in danger not only from animals that eat them. Sometimes bush grass fires come and burn the den. And sometimes when the stronger animals, like hyenas and lions, come, they kill the mother. Mother cheetahs don't have really big teeth or muscles like hyenas and lions, so they can't fight much. Without babies, they run away, but, of course, with babies, they don't run.

Hyena Paw Print

And sometimes the mothers have to go so far from the den to find food, they forget where the den is, or they're so weak from running after food they can't make it back. They just forget or abandon their babies.

So it's not exactly right to say Dooms didn't have a mother or father. We just didn't know where they were. And Dooms didn't know either. And that's why he was scared. And he had this look that I just told you about.

12

Because he was alone and scared, Mama and Daddy took Dooms home, and that was when he became a part of our family, even before I was.

When Dooms Was a Baby

Dooms stayed inside the house for the first three months of his life with us. That was because he couldn't have his shots yet for diseases like pneumonia which cats can get. Just like very small human babies who are too small for their shots, you have to be careful to keep them away from germs that cause diseases. For cheetahs, the problem is mostly with certain kinds of worms and bugs that

live in the grass. When the baby cheetah is drinking its mother's milk there is something right in the milk that blocks disease. But since Dooms was not getting cheetah's milk, only cow's milk, Mama and Daddy kept him away from the worms and bugs in the grass until he could get his shots.

Dooms drank cow's milk with water and an egg added—water, because cheetah's milk is much thinner than cow's milk, and egg, to make his coat shiny—and vitamins, some that were the same as if he were

eating the bones of animals. Slowly Dooms was given small bits of raw meat, and soon he ate almost all raw meat. When he grew up, Dooms ate only raw meat; he would never touch it cooked.

During the day, Dooms mostly slept and played with his sheepskin slipper. He'd jump all over the house when he was awake; onto the statues

19

on the stairs, onto the piano, the kitchen counters, everywhere. One day he jumped onto the table and ate a whole cheese!

Only once, Mama and Daddy gave Dooms a bath. He really hated it and spat and hissed and scratched everyone. That was Dooms's first and last bath. Even when Dooms was big and his tail dipped into the swimming pool when he was sitting on the edge, he would pull it out quickly and shake it off and look very cross. Cheetahs do not like water.

20

When Dooms Was Big, when I Knew Him

When Dooms was three months old, Mama and Daddy let him out of the house, and after that he was always outside. Outside close by, in the garden or under a tree. No one could ever see him in the grass because his fur and the grass were the same color. A gold color, with spots and dots of black. You might think it would be easy to see a cheetah's black spots, but somehow they look just like the thorn-bushes and rocks and anthills.

Each day he would walk out slowly in the morning sun, when the air was still cool, and find a nice tree to sleep under when the hot part of the day came. Dooms was lazy like that. Every once in a while he'd get

23

up, stretch, and yawn, and walk to one of his favorite high spots to look for some likely food. He liked the woodpile, or the ox-wagon we use to take everyone on hayrides when I have a birthday party by the dam, or sometimes a not-too-pointy anthill, which are not made by ants but by termites, which are called white ants here. My friend Davide, who helps take care of Dooms, eats the flying ants and even the big white queen ant, cooked, and I have even tried it—her—once. Quite tasty.

Dooms especially loved roofs of houses, the higher the better. When Dooms went up on our roof we'd try to get him down, because our roof is made of papyrus, or *marula* in the Swahili language, and papyrus is slippery and can be damaged by Dooms's claws. Papyrus is a kind of thick, hard grass that grows by the water in Africa. In Egypt, long ago, people

made boats of papyrus. When Daddy would try to get Dooms down off the roof, Dooms would get so mad that sometimes he'd swipe Daddy with his paw and Daddy would get a badly cut arm, all covered with blood. The roof Dooms really liked was the guest roof, maybe because it was round and pointed like an anthill. Once we had guests and in the morning they said to me, "Wasn't that a nice rain we had last night?" I knew it hadn't rained. Dooms had just been up there. I never told Mama and Daddy that.

Dooms's Friends

One night when Dooms was quite young, something like a teenager, we heard some noise outside and looked out and there was another cheetah. We thought it might be a friend for Dooms, but we

soon saw this was no friend. This was another male cheetah come to fight Dooms. Dooms rolled on his back and put his paws in the air and his head down to make himself look smaller, but the other cheetah was still growling and biting him. He soon bit a great hole in Dooms's ear, which he still has, and the whole thing was pretty nasty. The next night this new cheetah came again. Daddy tried to get him to go away, but he was determined to hurt Dooms.

The next night Mama and Daddy got a big

metal leopard cage and put a rabbit inside as bait, but the new cheetah

never went into the cage. That's just one example of how smart cheetahs

are. We were all still afraid the new cheetah would come again, but he didn't, so we were lucky. It wasn't long before Dooms grew big enough to defend his home territory without our help, which wasn't really much help.

Dooms really never had many friends, especially cheetah friends. When cheetahs are out in the bush, male cheetahs don't like to be friends, but we thought Dooms might find a girlfriend to mate with and have babies. We wanted the babies because there are not really very many cheetahs on earth now. There used to be a lot, on many continents, but now there are only cheetahs in Africa and even here there are not many. You see, people have been very greedy and killed cheetahs and used cheetahs' home grounds to plant food of

31

their own. Real thieves people are. I wonder where the cheetahs' homes are supposed to be when so many people steal their homes. This is what I wonder.

As I said, Dooms did not have many friends except us, of course, and the dogs. A giraffe and an eland came around quite a lot, but whenever Dooms

would go near them they'd run away. I guess that's natural when you think you'll be eaten. Anyway, there were really no friends for Dooms. Until Uni.

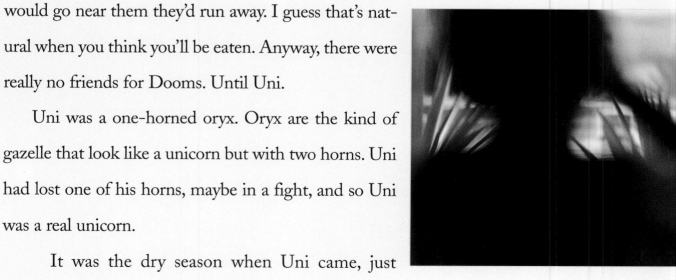

Uni was a one-horned oryx. Oryx are the kind of gazelle that look like a unicorn but with two horns. Uni had lost one of his horns, maybe in a fight, and so Uni was a real unicorn.

It was the dry season when Uni came, just

32

before the long April rains, and our garden had been eaten completely. The giraffe ate the tops of the thorn trees, the gazelle ate the cactuses, and Uni came to eat the rest.

When Uni first came into our garden, Dooms charged him, but when Uni charged back with his sword horn Dooms ran away. Dooms seemed pretty embarrassed, and he sat down close by and looked the other way to pretend he didn't notice Uni. This happened over and over for two or three days, and then Dooms and Uni settled down near each other and were friends.

Uni stayed eating our garden for eight days. We thought he might stay forever. We do see him out in the bush sometimes, but I'm not sure he recognizes us.

33

Dooms Learns to Find, Hunt, and Bring Down His Food

Dooms loved to play, and he was good at it. He could bat a soccer ball with his great paws, move it along the grass better than Michael Jordan, and then with one swipe bring it down where he'd guard it, with his claws, under his chin. Cheetahs' claws stay out all the time, they can't be drawn in like cats' claws, and when a cheetah is running the claws are just like the spikes or cleats on your sport shoes. Mama and Daddy said that Dooms playing with a

ball, or with Pupsor or Porgy, our dogs, was teaching him to hunt and bring down his food.

So Dooms played with us, or the dogs, but never the cats. Dooms hated cats. He terrorized the cats, chasing them up trees, and he went after them with real murder in his heart. I'm sorry to tell you that a few times he was able to get his heart's desire.

At first Dooms was not at all a good hunter. He would try to stalk, that is, sneak up on, Porgy or Pupsor, but he'd start from so far away they'd

always hear him coming and be off. He got a few rabbits and spring hares,

the animal that my dad calls the African kangaroo because it looks like a tiny kangaroo, but that was all. He never got anything bigger until he was about three years old. If Dooms had been with his mother, he'd still have drunk her milk until he was over a year old, and he'd have depended on her to bring home meat. That is why we didn't expect him to be a good hunter in the beginning.

Cheetahs are very fast, the fastest of all animals in fact, and they bring their food down by tripping or knocking over an animal when it's tired from running.

They do not depend on being powerful but on running fast and long.

That's why they have a small head to move through the wind easily and

40

strong legs and a long tail for balancing when they're running.

So you see, it wasn't until Dooms was larger and stronger that he could bring down a gazelle or an ostrich, his favorites. When I knew him, Dooms weighed nearly two hundred pounds and could bring down almost anything he liked.

Mama and Daddy said Dooms needed the wild food for all its small bones and skin and hair. And you know, even though we fed Dooms each night with five pounds of raw meat, he always went off every two weeks or so to hunt some wild food. He'd always

41

come back after these adventures with a fat stomach and a bloody mouth.
Always except once, when he didn't come back even after two days.

Or three or four or five days.
Every day Mama cried more, and
on the sixth day we stopped work
on the ranch and went out to try
and find our lost friend.

We drove our Land Rover to
all of Dooms's favorite places and
cupped our hands and called,
"Dooms, Dooms, Dooms," . . . but
our voices echoed back, and there was no Dooms. In the long grass under
the big sky, where could he be?

On the seventh day Daddy drove to Wami Ranch next door, where

Dooms was found once when he was a very young cheetah. That time he'd come to the ranch manager's house, walked into the dining room, and jumped onto the table, which was set for a dinner party. All the plates and cups and glasses fell off, even the white tablecloth and bowl of flowers. All to the floor. But Mrs.  Howard just laughed, she wasn't at all mad. She said it wasn't every day you had a cheetah come for dinner.

Anyway, we looked all over Wami Ranch, and there, at the top of the highest hill, where the radio tower is, Daddy stopped the car and called once more. And Dooms walked over and licked his leg. He'd been only a few feet away, but we couldn't see him.

When Daddy brought Dooms home that day, Mama cried and hugged him and said, "You naughty boy, don't you ever do that again."

44

Later that same day, Daddy went to Tanzania on business. Mama and I were upstairs getting ready to read and have a rest. What a day! It was the time Porgy and Dooms fought the Egyptian cobra snake.

An Egyptian cobra is a very big snake. This one was over seven feet long. I know this for sure because when Daddy came home later that day he held the snake over his head quite a long way, and my dad is over six feet tall. The snake was big and had long, pointed fangs you could easily see in its mouth. When it's angry, the Egyptian cobra spits poison, or venom, out of its mouth. It hopes this will go into your eyes. On either side of its head the Egyptian cobra has folds of skin that it spreads out, making its face look larger so as to scare its enemy (in this case Dooms and Porgy). I don't know about Dooms and Porgy, but we were scared all right. Porgy was in the cactus garden and had the snake in his mouth and was flinging it back and forth, all seven feet of it, and Dooms was running

around them, hissing. Mama looked out the window and screamed, "It's Porgy and Dooms and a snake. They'll be killed!"

With that we ran next door for help from Matheka, our cook, and were gone only a minute. But when we came back, Porgy was sitting next to the Egyptian cobra, which was lying on the grass like a prize. Mama thought the snake would finish off Porgy and Dooms, but Porgy finished the snake. Porgy-the-Snake-Killer! It was fantastic.

After that Matheka told us Porgy killed three more cobras and Dooms killed more, but we never knew for sure how many because we never saw them.

Any Day with Dooms

After Dooms established our house as his home territory, he wasn't bothered by any more male cheetahs. He spent his days eating, sleeping, playing, and being brushed and groomed. Every day one of us would brush him and we'd sit together and talk.

With Dooms you could talk about anything, ask him anything, and he knew the answers. He was the best listener I've ever seen. He'd quietly listen to whatever you wanted to say. One thing about Dooms, he was respectful of you, and he made sure you were respectful of him. It wasn't just his size. He was big, but it was more than that; it was the way he treated himself and you. He would not

accept you if you were not respectful. If you were silly and noisy, he might just walk away until you'd learned better. And if you were

disrespectful and mean and evil, he would stop you, with force if he had to. He would stare with a certain fierce look in his eyes, and he

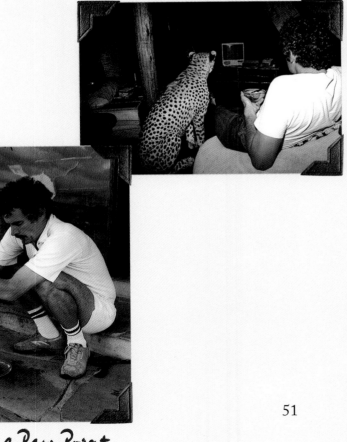

Making a Paw Print

51

would growl, as a threat. After that, if someone continued to act badly, he would strike. That's what I mean by demanding respect.

When Dooms was listening he'd just stare at you peacefully with his big yellow eyes. Eyes like the marbles in my collection. Big yellow glass marbles of eyes. He'd stare out far away on his plains and purr. When you brushed the short thick white hair under

his chin, he'd close his eyes and throw his head back with a low purr that some people thought was a growl but we knew was a purr. That was his favorite, to feel the warm sun and the dry cool air around him. This was enough for him. And enough for you.

When Dooms Got Sick ... and After

Dooms was never sick ... almost never. Not until that Tuesday in October, when the dry time had been very long and there was no tall grass left for Dooms to lie in and he still didn't want to move. He didn't want to eat either, or even drink his water. Mama drove into Nairobi that day and asked Dr. Richardson to come to us.

He came the next day and said maybe there was something inside Dooms that blocked his food from passing normally, something like a hair ball in a cat. He gave Dooms castor oil and said to keep in touch. But after two days Dooms wasn't better, and the doctor came again and tried some stronger medicine.

By Sunday Dooms was throwing up, even though there wasn't much to throw up, and Dr. Richardson came again. He said Dooms should be brought into the hospital in Nairobi for an X-ray to see what

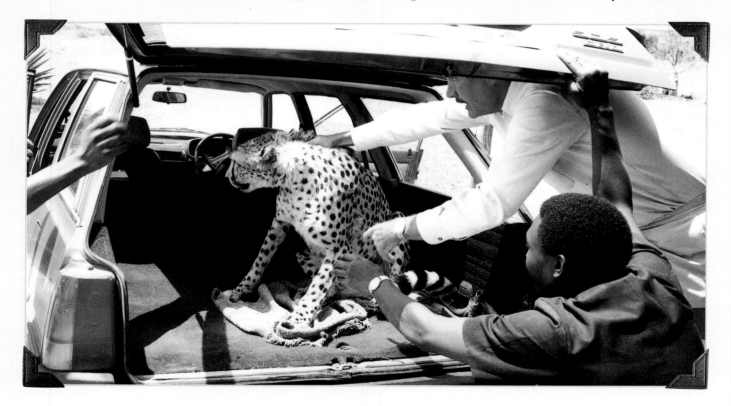

was in his stomach. Dooms had only been in a car twice before in his life, once coming back from Wami Ranch that time he ran away, and once when he was quite small and jumped through the picture window chasing cats. That time he was given a pill to calm him down. This time Dr. Richardson gave Dooms an injection that

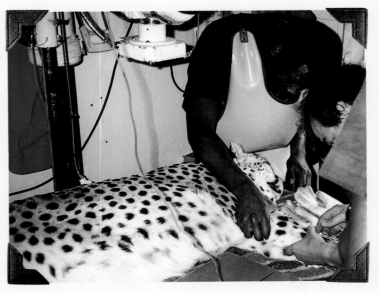

was something like the sleeping injection I got when I had my appendix out, but not as strong. Dooms didn't go to sleep, he just got a little quieter. Daddy and Mama and Matheka lifted Dooms on a blanket into the back of our station wagon. He still fought and hissed but not so much.

On the way to town Dooms seemed a bit sleepy, but he sat up and

59

looked around at everything like he had done before. Mama was worried about a possible operation, and she and Dr. Richardson talked about it. Maybe Dooms wouldn't have to have it. We couldn't tell until the X-ray. They talked like that all the way to Nairobi.

At the hospital we all helped to lift Dooms from the car to the X-ray table. The hospital workers were putting on their thick black gloves and the aprons they use to keep the X-rays out. Daddy had gone to move the car and Mama was still worried about the operation and wondering about it out loud and taking pictures of Dooms like she always did. You know how it is when you're doing something you think is important and you miss the thing that's really important. And so it was that we missed it when Death came in the door and stole Dooms.

We pushed Dooms's chest as if that would bring him back, pushed with all our might to keep his heart beating. Dr. Richardson was

sweating even though it wasn't a hot day. Mama was furious and screamed and shook her fists in the air and shouted, "No! No! No!" But Death would not listen and would not give Dooms back, so we took Dooms's body home.

We waited for three days, all of us hoping Death might change his mind. Mama went out several times each night to see if Death had returned Dooms to life. But after the third day we dug a hole in Dooms's favorite garden spot and put Dooms's body there forever. Mama and Daddy spoke prayers for Dooms's soul, and Davide, who was his very good friend, cried a lot.

For a few weeks after that, Dooms's soul did seem to remain with us, just a little off the ground, floating nearby. I thought I saw him many times in those weeks before he left to go high in the sky.

After Death took Dooms there was a black hole that I thought would never go away. It's hard to tell you about it. It was something like a big hole in your stomach that feels sore and sick. But I was wrong about it staying forever.

It was in April, half a year later, that Dr. Richardson came again. It was the first time he'd come since Dooms had left us, and when the car drove up I wondered why he was coming since we had no cheetah.

He opened the Land Rover door and I couldn't believe my eyes. There was a small cheetah, not a baby, but small and purring.

Her name is Shalla and she has soft fur and yellow eyes and a hard sandpaper tongue like Dooms. She even likes to lie in the same garden spot as Dooms did.

Perhaps Shalla and Dooms can see each other from there. I believe Dooms feels better knowing Shalla is with us. That's just my opinion.